Albert Schweitzer: Reverence for Life

ALBERT SCHWEITZER: REVERENCE

The Inspiring FOR LIFE

Words of a Great Humanitarian
With a Foreword

by Norman Cousins

Selected by Peter Seymour

Illustrated by Walter Scott

♛ *Hallmark Editions*

Contents

Foreword

Schweitzer's aim was not to dazzle an age but to awaken it, to make it comprehend that moral splendor is part of the gift of life, and that each man has unlimited strength to feel human oneness and to act upon it. He proved that although a man may have no jurisdiction over the fact of his existence, he can hold supreme command over the meaning of existence for him. Thus, no man need fear death; he need fear only that he may die without having known his greatest power—the power of his free will to give his life for others.

The individual in today's world feels cut off from the large forces or movements that determine his future. This leads to fatalism and default. Schweitzer demonstrated that one man can make a difference. He had no specific prescription or formula for the individual. All he hoped for was that the individual would be able to peel off the layers of hardened artificialities that separate him from his real self. Man's resources do not exist outside him. His responses must come from within. A thinking and feeling man is not a helpless man. The sense of paralysis proceeds not so much out of the mammoth size of the problem but out of the puniness of purpose.

It may be said that only a Schweitzer had the knowledge and personal power to answer satisfactorily the question: "What can one man do?" Certainly we can't all be Schweitzers. But what should concern us is not what it takes to be a Schweitzer but what it takes to be a man. Nature has not been equally lavish with her endowments, but each man has his own potential in terms of achievement and service. The awareness of that potential is the discovery of purpose; the fulfilment of that potential is the discovery of strength.

Norman Cousins

Albert Schweitzer: Reverence for Life

1/ The Story of My Life

Albert Schweitzer only wrote in detail about little more than the first half-century of his life. The following passages, from several of his books, create a chronological autobiography up to World War II:

I was born on January 14, 1875, at Kaysersberg in Upper Alsace, the second child of pastor Ludwig Schweitzer, who served a small evangelical congregation there. . . . A few weeks after my birth, my father came to Günsbach in the Münster Valley. There I lived a very happy childhood with my three sisters and a brother, troubled only by my father's frequent illnesses.

When I was five years old, my father began to instruct me on grandfather Schillinger's old piano. While he had no great technical ability, he improvised beautifully.

When I was seven I surprised my school teacher by playing on the harmonium some hymns for which I supplied my own harmonies. At eight I began to play the organ, although my legs were scarcely long enough to reach the pedals.

I attended the village school at Günsbach until the autumn of 1884. After that I was in the *Realschule* . . . at Münster for a year. During this time I took private lessons in Latin in order to prepare for the Fifth Form of the Gymnasium. In the autumn of 1885, I entered the Gymnasium at Mülhausen in Alsace.

On June 18, 1893, I passed the final examination. At the end of October, I enrolled in the University of Strasbourg. It was then in its prime. Chained by no traditions, teachers and students strove to realize the ideal of a modern university. . . . I attended lectures in the faculties of theology and philosophy.

In the year following April 1, 1894, I discharged my responsibilities for military service.

The years of study at Strasbourg passed quickly. At the end of the summer of 1897 I stood for the first theological examination.

On the advice of Theobald Ziegler, I next undertook the dissertation for the degree of doctor of philosophy. . . . Near the end of October, 1898, I traveled to Paris in order to study philosophy at the Sorbonne and to continue organ studies under Widor.

The doctoral research did not suffer damage either

from my devotion to art or from my social obligations, because my health permitted extensive studies at night. Sometimes I played for Widor in the morning without having been to bed.

In the summer of 1899, I was in Berlin and invested my time chiefly in philosophical studies. . . . Professor Heinrich Reimann, organist at the Kaiser Wilhelm Memorial Church, to whom I brought a letter of introduction from Widor, hired me as his substitute when he was away. Through him I came to know some Berlin musicians, painters, and sculptors.

On December 1, 1899, I secured an appointment as preacher at the Church of St. Nicholas in Strasbourg. First I was a so-called *"Lehrvikar."* When I passed my second theological examination, I became a curate.

My afternoon sermons, which I conceived as devotionals rather than as sermons, were so short that at one time certain groups in the congregation complained to Mr. Knittel, who held the post of "Inspector in Spiritual Matters." He had to summon me before him on this issue, but he was as embarrassed about it as I was. When he wanted to know what he was to say to those who felt themselves aggrieved, I responded that he should tell them that I was only a poor curate who stopped talking when he discovered he had nothing else to say about the text.

One distinct advantage of my position was that it left me adequate time for scientific work and music. . . . In this simple way the stream of my life flowed during the years which were so critical for my creative work. I worked at length and with unbroken concentration but without haste.

Since I had neither time nor money, I did not travel much. . . . When my savings allowed, I made the pilgrimage to Bayreuth when it was a festival year.

On July 21, 1900, my work on the problem of the Last Supper earned for me the degree of Licentiate in Theology. A second work, *The Secret of the Messiahship and the Passion,* secured for me in 1902 the position of *Privatdozent* at the University.

It was some conversations with students which moved me to my study of the history of research on the life of Jesus. They reported that they had not learned anything about previous research on this topic in their studies. . . . My *Quest of the Historical Jesus* appeared as early as 1906. While I was involved in this research, I completed in French my book on J. S. Bach.

In connection with the work on Bach, I published in the autumn of 1905, before my medical studies began, an essay on organ building. . . . I have given much time and energy to the struggle for the true organ. Many a night I have spent over organ plans which had to be approved or revised. And I have undertaken many a journey in order to study the question of restoring or rebuilding an organ. . . . How often were these many letters, journeys, and conversations in vain, because the people involved decided for the factory organ, whose plans looked so fine on paper!

The hardest fights were those in behalf of preserving old organs. . . . The first old organ which I saved—with much trouble—was the excellent work of Silberman at St. Thomas' in Strasbourg.

My friends used to say, "In the South he rescues old Africans, in the North old organs . . . ."

On Friday, October 13, 1905, I dropped some letters into a mailbox on the Avenue de la Grande Armée in Paris. They were addressed to my parents and to my friends. In them I said that I was going to become a medical student at the beginning of the winter semester and that I would later go as a doctor to Equatorial Africa. . . . The plan I now set in motion had been with me for a long time. Its origin was to be found in my student days. It was incomprehensible to me that I should lead a happy life when so many people around me were struggling with suffering and grief. . . . On a bright summer morning in the Whitsuntide holiday in 1896 at Günsbach, I awoke with the thought that my good fortune was not to be taken as something self-evident. . . . In peaceful reflection, while the birds were singing, I decided before I got up that I would be justified in devoting myself until I was thirty to science and art in order to give myself thereafter to direct services to humanity. . . . It was not yet clear to me what the exact nature of the activities I thus planned would be. I left it to circumstances to determine them. But one thing was certain. However insignificant it might appear, the goal must be a direct service of humanity.

What seemed most senseless to my friends was that I wanted to go to Africa as a physician, not a missionary. This meant at thirty years of age a long, difficult period of training. I had no doubt myself that the project would require an exceptional effort. . . . I wanted to be a doctor so I could serve without having to talk. . . . My calling as theological teacher and preacher was certainly a source of satisfaction to me. This new calling appeared to me, however, to be a matter of putting the religion of love to work rather than of talking about it.

It took him six years to complete his medical training. I took my last examination under Madelung, the surgeon. When I left the hospital to step into the cold darkness outside, I had difficulty appreciating that the tremendous effort of medical training was now behind me. Over and over, I had to assure myself that I was not dreaming but awake. As we walked along, Madelung's voice seemed to fall in from a great distance: "Only because of your good health were you able to finish that task."

Even while I was busy with my medical studies, I was making preparations for the journey to Africa. Early in 1912, I resigned from my teaching duties at the University and from my post at St. Nicholas'. . . .

To give up preaching and teaching represented a very great personal loss. . . . Finally I also gave up my residence on St. Thomas Embankment in order that with my wife—Helen Bresslau, daughter of the Strasbourg historian, whom I married on June 18, 1912—and I might spend my last months in my father's parsonage at Günsbach. . . .

I spent the spring of 1912 in Paris studying tropical medicine and purchasing things for Africa.

When I was sure I could summon the means for founding a small hospital, I made a definite offer to the Paris Missionary Society to come and serve at my own expense as a mission doctor at Lambaréné in its mission field on the River Ogowé. . . . About a year later, I had secured the funds necessary for the trip to Lambaréné and for the operation of the hospital during its first year. Some wealthy friends permitted me to think that they would again give help when my funds were exhausted.

In February, 1913, the seventy crates were prepared and sent as freight to Bordeaux. On the afternoon of Good Friday, 1913, my wife and I left Günsbach. In the evening of March 26, we embarked at Bordeaux.

At Lambaréné the missionaries cordially received us. . . . At first I had to make use of an old chicken house which stood next to our residence. In late autumn I was able to move into a corrugated-iron building with a palmleaf roof down by the river. Only eight meters long and four meters wide, it contained a small consulting room and an even smaller dispensary. Eventually there appeared around this unit a string of large bamboo huts for the native patients. The European patients were put up in the mission establishment and in the doctor's house.

Since my wife had been trained as a nurse, she was able to render service in the hospital. She did so courageously, caring for the dangerously ill. In addition, she handled the supply of linen and bandages and took care of the instruments in the dispensary. She made the preparations for the operations and administered the anesthetics. . . . It was a tremendous achievement for her to spend these hours in the hospital, while managing the complicated affairs of an African household.

The small amount of free time I had during my first year at Lambaréné was invested in the last three volumes of the American edition of Bach's organ music.

For my organ playing, I had the splendid piano with pedal attachment, built especially for the tropics, which the Paris Bach Society had given to me as a gift for my years of service as their organist. At first I was not in the mood to practice, for I had envisaged my African service as meaning the end of my career as an artist. Thus, I thought it would be easier to reconcile myself to this situation if I allowed my fingers and feet to lose their dexterity. But one evening as I was playing a Bach organ fugue, in a melancholy mood, the thought struck me that I could use my free hours in Africa for improving and deepening my technique. Immediately I conceived the plan of taking up in succession and learning in detail and by heart compositions by Bach, Mendelssohn, Widor, César Franck, and Max Reger, even if I had to spend weeks or months on a given piece.

My wife and I had now spent our second dry season in Africa. We were beginning to plan a return home at the beginning of the third when we heard, on August 5, 1914, that war had broken out in Europe. . . . Our health is not excellent, but it is not really bad. Tropical anemia has, of course, set in. It exhibits itself in intense fatigue. . . . In spite of the anemia and fatigue, I have been able to preserve my mental alertness. If the day has not been too much of a physical strain, I can spend two hours after supper on my work on ethics and culture in the history of human thought. . . . My desk stands before the lattice door which leads out on the veranda. Here I am able to get as much of the evening breeze as possible. The palms rustle lightly as the crickets and toads join in loud music. Harsh and strange cries issue from the forest. My faithful dog, Caramba, growls gently to make his presence known. A small dwarf antelope lies at my feet under the desk. In this solitude, I summon the thoughts which have been within me since 1900, in order to give some help in the restoration of culture. Solitude of the primeval forest!—how can I ever express my gratitude for what you have meant to me?

Schweitzer and his wife spent most of the war years un-molested at the hospital. He had received a great supply of medicines and dressings on the last ship to arrive be-fore the outbreak of the war, and was able to carry on work as usual. But when the rainy season of 1916-17 came, Mrs. Schweitzer's health faltered, and they had to leave the humid, sultry climate of Lambaréné and move to the coast. Then, suddenly . . .

In September, 1917 . . . the order came that we were im-mediately to be taken by ship to Europe and placed in a prisoner-of-war camp. Fortunately, the ship was several days late. With the aid of the missionaries and some Africans, we therefore had time to pack our medicines, instruments, and belongings in cases for storage in a small building of corrugated iron. . . .

Schweitzer and his wife were taken first to a prison camp at Garaison, in the Pyrenees. Although he was the only doctor among the prisoners, he was at first not al-lowed to help the sick. He managed to find a table, how-ever, at which he sat and practiced the organ "by using table as manual and floor as pedals."

They were moved to another camp in Provence. Schweitzer suffered from dysentery and his wife was ill much of the time. They were released in July of 1918 and went to live in Alsace, where the doctor spent his time with medical work and preaching. In 1919 a daughter, Rhena, was born. In 1920 Schweitzer lectured in Sweden. For several years he travelled, earning a living by writing and giving concerts. Then, in the winter of 1924 Albert Schweitzer returned to Lambaréné without his wife, whose health did not permit her to accompany him.

I had to make do with a few "volunteers" who came to the hospital as companions for the patients or were convalescents. They worked with no enthusiasm and, if it suited them, they found it convenient to disappear on their work days. . . .

The number of patients kept increasing. As a result, in 1924 and 1925 I sent to Europe for two doctors and two nurses.

In the autumn of 1925, the hospital was for the most part rebuilt. . . . Then a severe famine set in, because throughout the territory the cultivation of foods had been neglected for the cutting of timber. At the same time, we were afflicted by a terrible epidemic of dysentery . . . [which] proved to me that it was necessary to move the hospital to a larger site. . . . With great reluctance, then, I forced myself to move the hospital to a site three kilometers up the river where it could be expanded at will. Trusting in the support of friends of my work, I replaced the old bamboo huts, whose roofs were always needing repairs, with corrugated-iron structures. . . .

On January 21, 1927, when some of the buildings were complete, we transferred the patients to the new hospital. On the last trip that evening, I brought the mentally ill to the new site. Their caretakers never stopped telling them that in the new hospital they would be housed in cells with wooden floors. The old ones had floors of damp earth. . . . For the first time since I began work in Africa, my patients were provided for in a humane fashion! . . .

Doctor Schweitzer returned to Europe in 1927. Between then and 1939 he made two more trips to Lambaréné. When World War II broke out, he was again in Africa. Although we are constantly on the run, we are always preoccupied and oppressed by what we fear will come to pass. We feel ashamed that we have enough to eat here, while millions at a distance suffer from hunger. The news of those who are in prison camps, of the abuse of the Jews, and of the suffering which is endured by displaced people fills us with horror. . . . We know that we must seize courage from one another daily in order to go forward in the face of depression with the work which is given us to do. It continually strikes us as incomprehensible that we are called to a work of mercy, while others are condemned to suffering or must commit deeds which result in injury or death. This blessing daily gives us new energy for our tasks and makes them precious to us.

2/ Peace

Doctor Schweitzer remained in Lambaréné until 1948. From then until his death in 1965, at age ninety, he divided his time between Europe and Africa. In 1952 he was awarded the Nobel Peace Prize. Because he was involved in building a leper hospital in Lambaréné at the time, he did not deliver his Nobel speech until 1954. Two excerpts follow, as well as other writings on peace:

I believe that I voice the thoughts and hopes of millions of men who live in anxiety and in fear of future wars. May my words reach those who live on the other side of the barrier in the same anxiety as we do. May they receive my words in the sense in which they are offered.

Let those who hold the fates of peoples in their hands be careful to avoid everything which may worsen our situation and make it more perilous. Let them take to heart the marvelous words of the Apostle Paul: "As much as lies in you, be at peace with all men." They have meaning, not only for individuals, but also for nations. In their endeavors to preserve peace among themselves, may nations go to the uttermost limits of possibility, so that the human spirit may have time to develop, to grow strong, and to act!

In the name of all those who strive for peace, I venture to ask all peoples to take the first step along a new path. Not one will have to sacrifice a part of the authority and power he needs for self-preservation and defense.

Thus, if we make a beginning in the liquidation of the terrible war behind us, some measure of trust may arise among nations. Trust is the working-capital for all undertakings, without which nothing of real value can be accomplished. It provides the condition for beneficial developments in all spheres.

Today there is an absence of thinking which is characterized by a contempt for life. We waged war for questions which, through reason, might have been solved. No one won. The war killed millions of men, brought suffering to millions of men, and brought suffering and death to millions of innocent animals. Why? Because we did not possess the highest rationality of reverence for life. And because we do not yet possess this, every people is afraid of every other, and each causes fear to the others. We are mentally afflicted one for another because we are lacking in rationality. There is no other remedy than reverence for life, and at that we must arrive.

Only through a truly ethical civilization can life take on meaning. Only through it can mankind be saved from destruction, from its senseless and cruel wars. It alone can bring about peace in the world.

How did it come about that ethical ideas could not oppose the inhuman ideals of the war? It was due to the spirit of practical realism. I place at opposite extremes the spirit of idealism and the spirit of realism. The spirit of idealism means that men and women of the period arrive at ethical ideals through thinking, and that these ideals are so powerful that men say: We will use them to control reality. We will transform reality in accordance with these ideals. The spirit of idealism desires to have power over the spirit of realism. The spirit of practical realism, however, holds it false to apply ideals to what is happening. The spirit of realism has no power over reality. If a generation lives with these ideas, it is subject to reality. . . . What is characteristic of our age is that we no longer really believe in social or spiritual progress, but face reality powerless.

Trust is a matter of the spirit. It can be born only of the spirit. It can come about only when the spirit of reverence for life rises in all nations. Nations are not conscious of how inhumane they are. If they were, they would not rely on atomic weapons which can annihilate millions upon millions of people in a day.

All acts and facts are a product of spiritual power, the successful ones of power which is strong enough; the unsuccessful ones of power which is too weak. Does my behavior in respect of love affect nothing? That is because there is not enough love in me. Am I powerless against the untruthfulness and the lies which have their being all around me? The reason is that I myself am not truthful enough. Have I to watch dislike and ill will carrying on their sad game? That means that I myself have not yet completely laid aside small-mindedness and envy. Is my love of peace misunderstood and scorned? That means that I am not yet sufficiently peace-loving.

We are all subject to the mysterious and cruel law by which we maintain human life at the cost of other life. It is by this very destruction and harm of other life that we develop feelings of guilt. As ethical human beings, we must constantly strive to escape from this need to destroy—as much as we possibly can. We must try to demonstrate the essential worth of life by doing all we can to alleviate suffering. Reverence for life, which grows out of a proper understanding of the will to live, contains life-affirmation. It acts to create values that serve the material, the spiritual, and ethical development of man.

3/ Reverence for Life

*For much of his early life Albert Schweitzer was search-
ing for a meaningful definition for the "elementary and
universal concept of the ethical." Then, in 1915, while on
a river journey to attend a missionary's wife, Schweitzer
experienced a revelation:*

At sunset of the third day, near the village of Igendja,
we moved along an island set in the middle of the wide
river. On a sandbank to our left, four hippopotamuses
and their young plodded along in our same direction.
Just then, in my great tiredness and discouragement, the
phrase "Reverence for Life" struck me like a flash. As
far as I knew, it was a phrase I had never heard nor ever

read. I realized at once that it carried within itself the solution to the problem that had been torturing me. Now I knew that a system of values which concerns itself only with our relationship to other people is incomplete and therefore lacking in power for good. Only by means of reverence for life can we establish a spiritual and humane relationship with both people and all living creatures within our reach. Only in this fashion can we avoid harming others, and, within the limits of our capacity, go to their aid whenever they need us.

The philosophy of Reverence for Life follows from taking the world as it is. And the world means the horrible in the glorious, the meaningless in the full of meaning, the sorrowful in the joyful. However it is looked at it remains to many a riddle.

But that does not mean that we need stand before the problem of life at our wits' end, because we have to renounce all hope of comprehending the course of world events as having a meaning. Reverence for Life brings us into a spiritual relation with the world which is independent of all knowledge of the universe. Through the dark valley of resignation it leads us by an inward necessity up to the shining heights of ethical acceptance of the world.

On a stone on the river bank an old woman whose son had been taken sat weeping silently. I took hold of her hand and wanted to comfort her, but she went on crying as if she did not hear me. Suddenly I felt that I was crying with her, silently, towards the setting sun, as she was.

It is unthinkable that we civilized peoples should keep for ourselves alone the wealth of means for fighting sickness, pain, and death which science has given us. If there is any ethical thinking at all among us, how can we refuse to let these new discoveries benefit those who, in distant lands, are subject to even greater physical distress than we are? In addition to the medical men who are sent out by the governments, and who are never more than enough to accomplish a fraction of what needs doing, others must go out too, commissioned by human society as such. Whoever among us has through personal experience learned what pain and anxiety really are must help to ensure that those who out there are in bodily need obtain the help which came to him. He belongs no more to himself alone; he has become the brother of all who suffer. On the "Brotherhood of those who bear the mark of pain" lies the duty of medical work, work for humanity's sake. . . . Medical men must accomplish among the suffering in far-off lands, what is crying out for accomplishment in the name of true civilization.

A man must not try to force his way into the personality of another. To analyze others—unless it be to help back to a sound mind someone who is in spiritual or intellectual confusion—is a rude commencement, for there is a modesty of the soul which we must recognize, just as we do that of the body. The soul, too, has its clothing of which we must not deprive it, and no one has a right to say to another: "Because we belong to each other as we do, I have a right to know all your thoughts." Not even a mother may treat her child in that way. All demands of that sort are foolish and unwholesome. In this matter giving is the only valuable process; it is only giving that stimulates. Impart as much as you can of your spiritual being to those who are on the road with you, and accept as something precious what comes back to you from them.

Two things cast their shadows over my life. One is the thought that the world is inexplicably mysterious and full of misery. The other is that I have been born in a time of the spiritual decadence of mankind. I am, however, competent for handling both through the ethics of world-affirmation and life-affirmation which proceeds from the idea of reverence for life. In this way my life has been given firm foundation and clear direction.

Let me give you a definition of ethics: It is good to maintain life and further life; it is bad to damage and destroy life. However much it struggles against it, ethics arrives at the religion of Jesus. It must recognize that it can discover no other relationship of love. Ethics is the maintaining of life at the highest point of development—my own life and other life—by devoting myself to it in help and love, and both these things are connected.

We happen to believe that man's life is more important than any other form of which we know. But we cannot prove any such comparison of value from what we know of the world's development. True, in practice we are forced to choose. At times we have to decide arbitrarily which forms of life, and even which particular individuals, we shall save, and which we shall destroy. But the principle of reverence for life is none the less universal.

One realizes that he is but a speck of dust, a plaything of events outside his reach. Nevertheless, he may at the same time discover that he has a certain liberty, as long as he lives. Sometime or another all of us must have found that happy events have not been able to make us happy, nor unhappy events to make us unhappy. There is within each of us a modulation, an inner exaltation, which lifts us above the buffetings with which events assail us. Likewise, it lifts us above dependence upon the gifts of events for our joy. Hence, our dependence upon events is not absolute; it is qualified by our spiritual freedom. Therefore, when we speak of resignation it is not sadness to which we refer, but the triumph of our will to live over whatever happens to us. And to become ourselves, to be spiritually alive, we must have passed beyond this point of resignation.

Life-affirmation is the spiritual act in which a man begins to live reflectively and begins to give himself to his life with reverence in order to realize its true value. Life-affirmation is a deepening and an exaltation of the will to live.

The fundamental fact of human awareness is this: "I am life that wants to live in the midst of other life that wants to live." A thinking man feels compelled to approach all life with the same reverence he has for his own. Thus, all life becomes part of his own experience. From such a point of view, "good" means to maintain life, to further life, to bring developing life to its highest value.

A man is ethical only when life, as such, is sacred to him, that of plants and animals as that of his fellow men, and when he devotes himself helpfully to all life that is in need of help. Only the universal ethic of the feeling of responsibility in an ever-widening sphere for all that lives—only that ethic can be founded in thought. The ethic of the relation of man to man is not something apart by itself: it is only a particular relation which results from the universal one.

There slowly grew up in me an unshakable conviction

that we have no right to inflict suffering and death on another living creature unless there is some unavoidable necessity for it, and that we ought all of us to feel what a horrible thing it is to cause suffering and death out of mere thoughtlessness. And this conviction has influenced me only more and more strongly with time. I have grown more and more certain that at the bottom of our heart we all think this, and that we fail to acknowledge it and to carry our belief into practice chiefly because we are afraid of being laughed at by other people as sentimentalists, though partly also because we allow our best feelings to get blunted. But I vowed that I would never let my feelings get blunted, and that I would never be afraid of the reproach of sentimentalism.

At the station at Tarascon we had to wait for the arrival of our train in a distant goods shed. My wife and I, heavily laden with baggage, could hardly get along over the shingle between the lines. Thereupon a poor cripple whom I had treated in the camp came forward to help us. He had no baggage because he possessed nothing, and I was much moved by his offer, which I accepted. While we walked along side by side in the scorching sun, I vowed to myself that in memory of him I would in the future always keep a lookout at stations for heavily laden people, and help them. And this vow I have kept.

As I have come to know men, it has become clear to me

that many more idealistic desires are present among them than become visible. Just as the waters of the visible stream are small in comparison to those which flow underground, so is also the discernible idealism among men in comparison with that which is unreleased or just barely expressed in their hearts.

We must not allow cruel national thinking to prevail. The abolition of atomic weapons will become possible only if world opinion demands it. And the spirit needed to achieve this can be created only by reverence for life. The course of history demands that not only individuals become ethical personalities, but that nations do so as well.

The important thing is that we are part of life. . . . We possess the capacities to bring still other lives into existence. In the same way, if we look into a microscope we see cell producing cell. So nature compels us to recognize the fact of mutual dependence, each life necessarily helping the other lives which are linked to it. In the very fibers of our being, we bear within ourselves the fact of the solidarity of life. . . . Seeing its presence in ourselves, we realize how closely we are linked with others of our kind. We might like to stop here, but we cannot. Life demands that we see through to the solidarity of all life which we can in any degree recognize as having some similarity to the life that is in us.

4/ The Old Doctor

It may seem remarkable that Schweitzer, at age 30, de-
cided to enter medical school, and even more amazing
that he used his new profession to help the natives in
the jungles of Africa. But Schweitzer himself didn't
think so:

I had always supposed that I should go [to Africa] as
a doctor. In the early years, whenever there was building or similar material work to be done, I took pains to
pass it on to others who seemed to me fitted for it or
hired for that sort of work. Soon I had to admit that
this would not do. Either they did not appear, or they
were not qualified to forward the work. So I accustomed
myself to work which was very different from my medical duties. But the worst came later. In the closing
months of 1925, a great famine endangered my hospital,
and I was forced to lay out a plantation for the hospital so
that in any future period of famine we might be able to
keep our heads in some measure above water. I had to
superintend the clearing of the jungle myself. The motley
array of voluntary workers assembled from among those
who attended the patients would recognize no authority
but that of the "Old Doctor," as I was called there. So
for weeks and months I stood in the jungle trying to

wrest fruitful land from it, and tormented by unruly workers. Whenever I was in complete despair, I thought of Goethe, who had imagined his Faust, in the end, busily regaining land from the sea where men might live and find nourishment.

At the beginning of my service, I was greatly troubled because I could not find natives to serve as interpreters and orderlies. The first one who proved to be of any help had formerly been a cook. . . . He remained with me in spite of the fact that I could not pay him as much as he received in his former work. Moreover, he gave me some very good advice about dealing with Africans. On one point, which seemed most important to him, I could not follow through. He told me to refuse to treat the persons whose lives I was not likely to save. Repeatedly he pointed to the example of the fetish doctors, who turned aside such cases so that their reputations would not be jeopardized. . . .

To induce the natives to submit to operations needed no great skill in persuasion from me. A few years before a Government doctor, Jauré-Guibert by name, had stayed for a short time at Lambaréné on one of his journeys and performed some successful operations, on the strength of which my very modest surgical skill met with a trustful reception. Fortunately I did not lose a single one of those patients on whom I first operated.

So far as the rule could be carried out, I used to exact from my native patients some tangible evidence of their gratitude for the help they had received. Again and again I used to remind them that they enjoyed the blessing of the hospital because so many people in Europe had made sacrifices to provide it; it was, therefore, now on their part a duty to give all the help they could to keep it going. Thus I gradually got it established as a custom that in return for the medicines given I received gifts of money, bananas, poultry, or eggs. What thus came in was, of course, far below the value of what had been received, but it was a contribution to the upkeep of the hospital. With the bananas I could feed the sick whose provisions had given out, and with the money I could buy rice, if the supply of bananas failed. I also thought that the natives would value the hospital more if they had to contribute to its maintenance themselves according to their ability, than if they simply got everything for nothing.

In addition to the physicians who are sent out by European governments and who can accomplish only a part of what is required, others must go also, commissioned by the human community as such. Those of us who through our experience have come to know what pain and anxiety are must endeavor to extend to others in physical distress the sort of help we have received. We are no longer our own—we are brothers to all who suffer.

5/ Religion and Ethics

Trained in theology and philosophy, Schweitzer spent much of his early life, and a good deal of time in his latter years, concerned with the meaning and purpose of religion. He wrote extensively, too, on the life of Jesus, Whose person and ethics Schweitzer reflected with almost divine clarity:

The belief in the Kingdom of God is the most difficult demand Christian faith makes of us. We are asked to believe in what seems impossible, namely in the victory of the spirit of God over the spirit of the world. Our trust and hope are invested in the miracle which the spirit can produce.

But the miracle must occur in us before it occurs in the world. We dare not hope that by our efforts we can create the conditions of the kingdom in the world. We must certainly work for it. But there can be no divine kingdom in the world, if there is not one first of all in our hearts. The beginning of the kingdom is to be found in our determination to bring our every thought and deed under the dominion of the kingdom. Nothing will come to pass without inwardness. The spirit of God will only contend against the spirit of the world when it has triumphed over that spirit in our hearts.

Why did the idea of the Kingdom of God have no significance in the early church? It was closely connected with the expectation of the end of the world. And when hope of the coming of the end of the world had faded, the idea of the Kingdom of God lost its force as well. So it came about that the creeds were not at the same time preoccupied with the idea of redemption. Only after the Reformation did the idea gradually arise that we men and women in our own age must so understand the religion of Jesus that we endeavor to make the Kingdom of God a reality in this world. It is only through the idea of the Kingdom of God that religion enters into relationship with civilization.

Three times a week, from eleven to twelve, when the morning lessons were over, I had to take the Confirmation classes for boys, which in Alsace continue for two years. I tried hard to give them as little homework to do as possible, that the lessons might be a time of pure refreshment for heart and spirit. I therefore used the last ten minutes for making them repeat after me, and so get to know by heart, Bible sayings and verses of hymns which they might take away from these classes to guide them throughout their lives. The aim of my teaching was to bring home to their hearts and thoughts the great truths of the Gospel, and to make them religious in such a way that in later life they might be able to resist the temptations to irreligion which would assail them. I tried also to awake in them a love for the Church, and a feeling of need for a solemn hour for their souls in the Sunday services. I taught them to respect traditional doctrines, but at the same time to hold fast to the saying of St. Paul that where the spirit of Christ is, there is liberty.

Of the seed which for years I was thus sowing, some has taken root and grown, as I have been privileged to learn. Men have thanked me for having then brought home to their hearts the fundamental truths of the religion of Jesus as something to be absorbed into one's thought, and having thus strengthened them against the danger of giving up all religion in later life.

We must take the ethical religion of Jesus out of the setting of His world-view and put it in our own. Whereas He expected the Kingdom of God to come at the end of the world, we must endeavor, under the influence of the spirit of His ethical religion, to make the Kingdom of God a reality in this world by works of love.

The ethics of materialism is unnecessary. Society has no need that the individual should serve it. Society does not need his morality; it can force upon him the sociology which it holds to be best. Herbert Spencer was not only a great thinker but a great prophet. He expressed anxiety lest the state should by violence force the individual to submit to it. He was right. The ethics of materialism has not triumphed, for in our days we have experienced the state destroying the individual in order to make the individual its servant. Therefore, the ethics of materialism is no religion.

The Sermon on the Mount is the unassailable charter of liberal Christianity. By the authority of Jesus, the truth that the essence of religion is ethical is established.

Moreover, due to the withering of the late Jewish eschatological world-view, Jesus' religion of love has been freed from the dogmatism in which it was clothed.

The mold into which the casting was poured is shattered.

Now we are free to let the religion of Jesus come alive in our thought in its direct spiritual and ethical character. We know that much which is valuable has been carried to us in ecclesiastical Christianity, garbed in Greek dogmas and kept alive by the piety of many centuries. We, therefore, hold to the church in love, reverence, and gratitude.

But while hers, we are men who appeal to the words of Paul, "Where the spirit of the Lord is, there is freedom," believing that we serve Christianity better by our devotion to Jesus' religion of love than by submitting to all the articles of faith. If the church possesses the spirit of Jesus, there is ample room in her for every form of Christian piety, even for that which will be free.

The religion of our age gives the same impression as an African river in the dry season—a great river bed, sand banks, and between, a small stream which seeks its way. One tries to imagine that a river once filled that bed; that there were no sand banks but that the river flowed majestically on its way; and that it will someday be like that again. Is it possible, you say, that once a river filled this bed? Was there a time when ethical religion was a force in the spiritual life of the time? Yes, in the eighteenth century. Then ethical religion and thinking formed one unity. Thinking was religious, and religion was a thinking religion. Because it was conditioned by ethical religious ideas, the thinking of that period undertook to represent reality to itself as it should be. It possessed ethical ideals in accordance with which it transformed reality.

From my youth I have been convinced that all religious truth must be conceived as truth which can necessarily be understood. In the field where ideas struggle with one another and where religions enter into contest with one another, Christianity cannot plead for special treatment. It must be in the thick of the battle of ideas, trusting in the power of its inherent truth.

6/ Respect for Animals

Doctor Schweitzer's reverence for life included all living things, and from an early age he felt a strong concern for the plight and treatment of animals. In the following selections he expresses his deep feelings about animals:

One thing that specially saddened me was that the unfortunate animals had to suffer so much pain and misery. The sight of an old limping horse, tugged forward by one man while another kept beating it with a stick to get it to the knacker's yard at Colmar, haunted me for weeks.

It was quite incomprehensible to me—this was before I began going to school—why in my evening prayers I should pray for human beings only. So when my mother had prayed with me and had kissed me good night, I used to add silently a prayer that I had composed myself for all living creatures. It ran thus: "O heavenly Father, protect and bless all things that have breath; guard them from all evil, and let them sleep in peace."

It was spring and the end of Lent, when one morning my friend said to me, "Come along, let's go on to the Rebberg and shoot some birds." This was to me a terrible proposal, but I did not venture to refuse for fear he should laugh at me. We got close to a tree which was still without any leaves, and on which the birds were singing beautifully to greet the morning, without showing the least fear of us. Then stooping like a red Indian hunter, my companion put a bullet in the leather of his catapult and took aim. In obedience to his nod of command, I did the same, though with terrible twinges of conscience, vowing to myself that I would shoot directly after he did. At that very moment the church bells began to ring, mingling their music with the songs of the birds and the sunshine. It was the warning-bell, which began half an hour before the regular peal-ringing, and for me it was a voice from heaven. I shooed the birds away, so that they flew where they were safe .... and then I fled home. And ever since then, when the Passiontide bells ring out to the leafless trees and the sunshine, I reflect with rush of grateful emotion how on that day their music drove deep into my heart the commandment: "Thou shalt not kill."

I have twice gone fishing with rod and line just because other boys asked me to, but this sport was soon made impossible for me by the treatment of the worms that were put on the hook for bait, and the wrenching of the mouths of the fishes that were caught. I gave it up, and even found courage enough to dissuade other boys from going.

I have the virtue of caring for all stray monkeys that come to our gate. (If you have had any experience with large numbers of monkeys, you know why I say it is a virtue thus to take care of all comers until they are old enough or strong enough to be turned loose, several together, in the forest—a great occasion for them—and for me!) Sometimes there will come to our monkey colony a wee baby monkey whose mother has been killed, leaving this orphaned infant. I must find one of the older monkeys to adopt and care for the baby. I never have any difficulty about it, except to decide which candidate shall be given the responsibility. Many a time it happens that the seemingly worst-tempered monkeys are most insistent upon having this sudden burden of foster parenthood given to them.

A friend in Hanover owned a small café. He would daily throw out crumbs for the sparrows in the neighbor-

hands of enterprises that will develop their values.

When in the spring the withered grey of the pastures gives place to green, this is due to the millions of young shoots which sprout up freshly from the old roots. In like manner the revival of thought which is essential for our time can only come through a transformation of the opinions and ideals of the many brought about by individual and universal reflection about the meaning of life and of the world.

The formation of drops of rain, of snowflakes, and of hailstones had always been a special puzzle to me. It hurt me to think that we never acknowledge the absolutely mysterious character of Nature, but always speak so confidently of explaining her, whereas all that we have really done is to go into fuller and more complicated descriptions, which only make the mysterious more mysterious than ever. . . . It became clear to me that what we label Force or "Life" remains in its own essential nature forever inexplicable.

The effort for harmony never succeeds. Events cannot be harmonized with our activities. Working purposefully toward certain ends, we assume that the Creative Force in the world is doing likewise. Yet, when we try to define its goal, we cannot do so. It tends toward developing a type of existence, but there is no coordinated, definite end to be observed, even though we think there should be. We like to imagine that Man is nature's goal; but facts do not support that belief.

When we consider the immensity of the universe, we must confess that man is insignificant. The world began, as it were, yesterday. It may end tomorrow. Life has existed in the universe but a brief second. And certainly man's life can hardly be considered the goal of the universe. Its margin of existence is always precarious. Study of the geologic periods shows that. So does the battle against disease. When one has seen whole populations annihilated by sleeping sickness, as I have, one ceases to imagine that human life is nature's goal. In fact, the Creative Force does not concern itself about preserving life. It simultaneously creates and destroys. Therefore, the will-to-live is not to be understood within the circle of Creative Force. Philosophy and religion have repeatedly sought the solution by this road; they have projected our will to perfection into nature at large, expecting to see its counterpart there. But in all honesty we must confess that to cling to such a belief is to delude ourselves.

The purpose of all philosophy is to make us aware as thinking beings of the intelligent and intimate relationship with the universe in which we have to stand, and of the way in which we must behave in the presence of the

49

stimuli that come from it.

One kind of philosophy is able to bring man and the universe together only by doing violence to nature and the world and by forcing the world into harmony with man's thought.

The other, the insignificant nature philosophy, leaves the world and nature as they are, and compels man to find himself and assert himself in them as a spiritually and creatively triumphant being. The first philosophy is ingenious, the second elementary. . . . The first philosophy has its day and disappears. The second, the plain and simple nature philosophy, remains . . . it is our appointed task to bring it to an affirmative position in relation to the world and life, in so simple a fashion that all thoughtful people throughout the world would have to share in this thinking, and therein find peace with the infinite and incentive for creative activity. . . .

There is in each of us the will-to-live, which is based on the mystery of what we call "taking an interest." We cannot live alone. Though man is an egoist, he is never completely so. He *must* always have some interest in life about him. If for no other reason, he must do so in order to make his own life more perfect. Thus it happens that we want to devote ourselves; we want to take our part in perfecting our ideal progress; we want to give meaning to the life in the world. This is the basis of our striving for harmony with the spiritual element.

8/ The Music Lover

Among Schweitzer's many interests was music. He not only played the organ but became an expert on organ building. Following are some of his writings on music, including part of an essay on Johann Sebastian Bach:

The drive to express poetic and pictorial thoughts is the essence of music. Music is an invitation to the creative imagination of the hearer to make alive the feelings and the visions from which it is derived. But this can only come to pass, if he who speaks in the language of sound possesses the mysterious capacity of rendering thought clearly and vividly.

Bach commands a language of sound. His music is a vehicle of recurring rhythmical motives, voicing peaceful happiness, living joy, intense pain, or misery sublimely met.

His music is poetic and pictorial because its themes are born of poetic and pictorial ideas. From these themes, the composition is developed, an architectural structure of lines of tones. The pictorial and poetic music reveals itself as Gothic architecture in sound. The greatest thing about the elemental vitality, majestic plasticity, and structural perfection we find in Bach's music is the spirit which permeates the whole. In this music a soul which seeks for peace amid the world's unrest and has, indeed, already tasted this blessing permits others to share its experience.

I was curiously affected by the organs which were built toward the end of the nineteenth century. Although they were lauded as miracles of advanced technical skill, I could find no pleasure in them. In the autumn of 1896, I made my way home after my first visit to Bayreuth, via Stuttgart, in order to examine the new organ in the *Liederhalle* of that town, about which the newspapers had published enthusiastic reports. Herr Lang, the organist of the Stiftskirche, who both as musician and as man stood in the first rank, was kind enough to show it to me. When I heard the harsh tone of the much belauded instrument, and in the Bach fugue which Lang played to me perceived a chaos of sounds in which I could not distinguish the separate voices, my foreboding that the modern organ meant in that respect a step not forward but backward, suddenly became a certainty. In order to convince myself finally of this fact and to find the reasons for it, I used my free time in the next few years in getting to know as many organs, old and new, as possible. I also discussed the matter with all the organists

and organ builders with whom I came in contact . . . .
The work and the worry that fell to my lot through the practical interest I took in organ building, made me sometimes wish that I had never troubled myself about it, but if I do not give it up, the reason is that the struggle for the good organ is to me a part of the struggle for truth. And when on Sundays I think of this or that church in which a noble organ is sounding because I saved it from an ignoble one, I feel myself richly rewarded for all the time and trouble which in the course of over thirty years I have sacrificed in the interests of organ building.

Together with my veneration for Bach went the same feeling for Richard Wagner. When I was a schoolboy at Mülhausen at the age of sixteen, I was allowed for the first time to go to the theater, and I heard there Wagner's *Tannhäuser*. This music overpowered me to such an extent that it was days before I was capable of giving proper attention to the lessons in school.

In Strasbourg, where the operatic performances conducted by Otto Lohse were of outstanding excellence, I had the opportunity of becoming thoroughly familiar with the whole of Wagner's works, except, of course, *Parsifal*, which at that time could only be performed at Bayreuth. It was a great experience for me to be present in Bayreuth in 1896, at the memorable first repetition of the Tetralogy since the original performances in 1876.

9/ Humanity to Man

Behind and below Dr. Schweitzer's profound ethical concerns lay a deep and basic love for his fellow men. In these final selections from his writings he comes close to the heart of his faith:

Of those who feel any sort of impulse, and would prove actually fitted, to devote their lives to independent personal activity, the majority are compelled by circumstances to renounce such a course. As a rule this is because they have to provide for one or more dependents, or because they have to stick to their calling in order to earn their own living. Only one who thanks to his own ability or the devotion of friends is in worldly matters a free man, can venture nowadays to take the path of independent activity. This was not so much the case in earlier times because anyone who gave up remunerative work could still hope to get through life somehow or other, while anyone who thought of doing the same in the difficult economic conditions of today would run the risk of coming to grief not only materially but spiritually as well.

I am compelled, therefore, not only by what I have observed, but by experience also, to admit that worthy and capable persons have had to renounce a course of independent action which would have been of great value to the world, because circumstances rendered such a course impossible.

Those who are so favored as to be able to embark on a course of free personal activity must accept this good fortune in a spirit of humility. They must often think of those who, though willing and capable, were never in a position to do the same. And as a rule they must temper their own strong determination with humility. They are almost always destined to have to seek and wait till they find a road open for the activity they long for. Happy are those to whom the years of work are allotted in richer measure than those of seeking and waiting! Happy those who in the end are able to give themselves really and completely!

Anyone who proposes to do good must not expect people to roll stones out of his way, but must accept his lot calmly if they even roll a few more upon it. A strength which becomes clearer and stronger through its experience of such obstacles is the only strength that can conquer them. Resistance is only a waste of strength.

Create for yourselves an auxiliary task, a simple and, if possible, a secret one. Open your eyes and try to see where a man needs a little time, a little sympathy, a little company, a little care. Perhaps he is a solitary, an embittered, a sick or an awkward man, to whom you can mean something. Perhaps he is an old man, perhaps a child. Who can enumerate all the possible uses of the valuable operating capital called man? He is needed in all parts. Therefore seek you for an opportunity to set your humanity to work. Do not avoid an auxiliary task, in which you give of yourself as man to other men. One is surely destined for you if you but really want it.

In my own life anxiety, trouble, and sorrow have been allotted to me at times in such abundant measure that had my nerves not been so strong, I must have broken down under the weight. Heavy is the burden of fatigue and responsibility which has lain upon me without a break for years. I have not much of my life for myself, not even the hours I should like to devote to my wife and child.

But I had blessings too: that I am allowed to work in the service of mercy; that my work has been successful; that I receive from other people affection and kindness in abundance; that I have loyal helpers, who identify themselves with my activity; that I enjoy a health which allows me to undertake most exhausting work; that I have a well-balanced temperament which varies little, and an energy which exerts itself with calmness and deliberation; and finally, that I can recognize as such whatever happiness falls to my lot, accepting it also as a thing for which some thank offering is due from me.

I feel it deeply that I can work as a free man at a time when an oppressive lack of freedom is the lot of so many, as also that though my immediate work is material, yet I have at the same time opportunities of occupying myself in the sphere of the spiritual and intellectual.

That the circumstances of my life provide in such varied ways favorable conditions for my work, I accept as something of which I would fain prove myself worthy.

In my first years at Mülhausen I suffered much from a homesick longing for the church of Günsbach; I missed my father's sermons, and the services I had been familiar with all my life.

The sermons used to make a great impression on me, because I could see how much of what my father said in the pulpit was of a piece with his own life and experience. I came to see what an effort, I might say what a struggle, it meant for him to open his heart to the people every Sunday. I still remember sermons I heard from him while I was at the village school.

But what I loved best was the afternoon service, and of these I hardly ever missed a single one when I was in Günsbach. In the deep and earnest devotion of those services the plain and homely style of my father's preaching showed its real value, and the pain of thinking that the holy day was now drawing to its close gave these services a peculiar solemnity.

From the services in which I joined as a child I have taken with me into life a feeling for what is solemn, and a need for quiet and self-recollection, without which I cannot realize the meaning of my life. I cannot, therefore, support the opinion of those who would not let children take part in grown-up people's services till they to some extent understand them. The important thing is not that they shall understand, but that they shall feel something of what is serious and solemn. The fact that the child sees his elders full of devotion, and has to feel something of their devotion himself, that is what gives the service its meaning for him.

We ought all to make an effort to act on our first thoughts and let our unspoken gratitude find expression. Then there will be more sunshine in the world, and more power to work for what is good. But as concerns ourselves we must all of us take care not to adopt as part of our theory of life all people's bitter sayings about the ingratitude in the world. A great deal of water is flowing underground which never comes up as a spring. In that thought we may find comfort. But we ourselves must try to be the water which does find its way up; we must become a spring at which men can quench their thirst for gratitude.

10/ Important Dates in the Life of Albert Schweitzer

1875   Born January 14 at Kayersberg, Upper Alsace; grows up in Günsbach.

1893   Enters Strasburg University; becomes organist in that city.

1894   Year of military service.

1899   Receives Doctorate in Philosophy.

1900   Receives Doctorate in Theology.

1903   Becomes Principal of Theological College in Strasburg.

1906   Enters medical school; publishes *The Quest of the Historical Jesus* and pamphlet on organ building.

1912   Completes medical training; marries Hélène Bresslau.

1913   Goes to Africa; founds hospital at Lambaréné.

1917-18   Prisoner of war.

1919-22   Teaching, lecturing, writing in Europe.

1921   Publishes *On the Edge of the Primeval Forest*.

1923   Returns to Africa and Lambaréné.

1928   Receives Goethe Prize in recognition of "Service to Humanity."

1952   Receives the Nobel Peace Prize.

1958   Publishes *Peace or Atomic War*.

1965   Dies September 4, at Lambaréné.

Set in Linotype Aldus, a Roman with old-face characteristics, designed by Hermann Zapf. Aldus was named for the 16th century Venetian printer Aldus Manutius. Typography by Joseph Thuringer and set at Rochester Typographic Service.
Printed on Hallmark Eggshell Book paper.
Designed by William M. Gilmore.